NOAH AND THE ARK

Retold by Anne de Graaf   Illustrated by José Pérez Montero

B&H
BROADMAN
& HOLMAN
PUBLISHERS

NOAH AND THE ARK

Published in 1998 by Broadman & Holman Publishers,
Nashville, Tennessee

Text copyright © 1998 Anne de Graaf
Illustration copyright © 1998 José Pérez Montero
Design by Ben Alex
Conceived, designed and produced by Scandinavia Publishing House

Printed in Singapore
ISBN 0-8054-1781-8

*Dedicated to José Pérez Montero's future grandchildren
and to Julia de Graaf*

A long, long, long, long time ago, no one said, *"Thank You"* to God anymore.

Everyone chose to be bad and this made God very sad. One man was different. His name was Noah. He talked and listened to God. He thanked God for His love.

Name all the things and people you can thank God for.

God told Noah, "There will be a huge flood. Build a boat. Build a BIG boat. Build a VERY BIG boat!" Noah's neighbors laughed at Noah. "We live in the desert! Where's your water?"

Who did Noah listen to?
Who do you listen to?

God said to fill the boat, the BIG boat, the VERY BIG boat with two of every animal. God promised to keep Noah and his family and the animals safe.

11

Then it started to rain and rain. It rained for forty days and forty nights. All those animals! All those days and nights! All that rain!

Noah's ark floated higher and higher, higher even than the mountaintops. As water covered the earth, all the living things drowned.

When the rain stopped,
God sent a wind.

Make a sound like the rain. Now make a sound like the wind.

15

Noah sent out a
raven to see if he
could find dry
land. But it was
too early.

Can you
make flapping
sounds like the
raven's wings?

es go, but he came back. When
e dove returned with an olive leaf in
ewhere there were places dry enough

A week later Noah sent out the dove a
didn't come back, Noah knew it had fo
Noah took the roof off the ark.

d time. When the dove
a place to land. Then

God said to Noah, "You, your family, and all the animals may leave the boat. Go onto the land and build homes."

Back on land, Noah and
his family built a place to
thank God for keeping

His promise, for keeping them
safe. Then God gave Noah a gift.

*Turn the page
and see the
present. . . .*

God gave Noah the present of
another promise. God was so happy
that Noah said *"thank you."*

He promised three things.
First, He would never flood the earth
again. Second, there would always be
seasons of the year.

After autumn would come winter and after winter would come spring . . .

... *and after spring would come summer.*

The third part of God's promise
was that day would follow night.

Then God made something very special. Using every color, He made the first rainbow. "As a sign of My promise, I have set My rainbow in the clouds."

What colors are in the rainbow? Light blue, light-light blue. . . .

God always keeps
His promises.

Just like the colors are endless, so the rainbow is endless. And just like the rainbow, God's love goes on and on and on. . . .

A NOTE TO THE Big PEOPLE:

The *Little Children's Bible Books* may be your child's first introduction to the Bible, God's Word. In *Noah and the Ark*, detailed illustrations make chapters six through nine of Genesis spring to life. This is a DO book. Point things out and ask your child to find, seek, say, and discover.

Before you read these stories, pray that your child's little heart would be touched by the love of God. These stories are about planting seeds, having vision, learning right from wrong, and choosing to believe.

A little something fun is said in italics by the narrating animal, to make the story come alive. In this DO book, wave, wink, hop, moo, or do any of the other things the stories suggest so this can become a fun time of growing closer. Pray together after you read this. There's no better way for big people to learn from little people.

A NOTE TO THE LITTLE PEOPLE:

Someone very special gave you this book. It is a special book, and it was given to someone even more special . . . and that's you.

This may be your first Bible. The Bible brings you closer to God. Even closer. Why even closer? Because Jesus said the angels of the little ones (that's you) are the closest to God.

There are lots of fun things to do when you hear these stories. Listen closely. Your job is to make sure the someone special who reads to you does these fun things with you. After that, you can both close your eyes and thank Jesus for being together. There's no better way for little people to learn from big people.